JONAH
AND THE GREAT FISH

RETOLD AND ILLUSTRATED BY WARWICK HUTTON

A MARGARET K. MCELDERRY BOOK

ATHENEUM   1983   NEW YORK

Library of Congress Cataloging in Publication Data

Hutton, Warwick.
Jonah and the great fish.
"A Margaret K. McElderry Book."
Summary: Retells the Biblical story of how a man
was swallowed up by a great fish.
1. Jonah (Biblical prophet)—Juvenile literature.
2. Bible stories, English—O.T. Jonah.   [1. Jonah
(Biblical prophet) 2. Bible stories—O.T.]   I. Title.
BS580.J55H87   1984   224'.9209505   83-15477
ISBN 0-689-50283-4

Published simultaneously in Canada by McClelland & Stewart, Ltd.
Manufactured by Dai Nippon Printing Company in Japan
First Edition

for Cailey and Marlene

Long ago there lived a man called Jonah. One day he heard the voice of the Lord calling to him, and it said, "Arise and go to the city of Nineveh. The people there are wicked. You must preach and persuade them to give up their evil ways."

Jonah was frightened by the Lord's command. So he fled from the presence of the Lord, down to the port of Joppa.

There, in the harbor, he found a ship that was about to sail to far-off Tarshish. He paid his fare and went on board, hoping to escape from the presence of the Lord.

The ship set sail, but almost at once the Lord sent out a
great wind into the sea, and there was a mighty tempest. The
wind and the waves grew ever more threatening.

The sailors were afraid and they threw the cargo into the sea to lighten the ship.

All this time, Jonah, weary and worn, lay fast asleep. The captain woke him angrily. "Arise, O sleeper! Call upon your God to save us!"

The sailors believed that someone on board had brought bad luck to the ship. "Come and draw lots, so we may know who is causing this evil," they said. Jonah drew the black stick. Then they knew that he was the cause of their trouble.

So Jonah rose up and told them that he had feared the Lord's command and had fled from his presence.

The sailors were afraid. "What shall we do with you, Jonah, so that the sea will be calm again?" And Jonah answered, "Throw me into the the sea. Only then will the waters be calm. I know that this great storm is upon us because of me."

Nevertheless, the sailors worked hard to bring the ship safely to land, but they could not. The sea was too rough and the winds were against them. They lost their oars and their sail.

In despair, they begged Jonah to forgive them. Then they lifted him up and threw him into the sea.

At once, the wind stopped raging, and the sea grew calm.

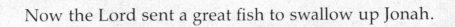

Now the Lord sent a great fish to swallow up Jonah.

And Jonah was in the belly of the fish for three days and three nights.

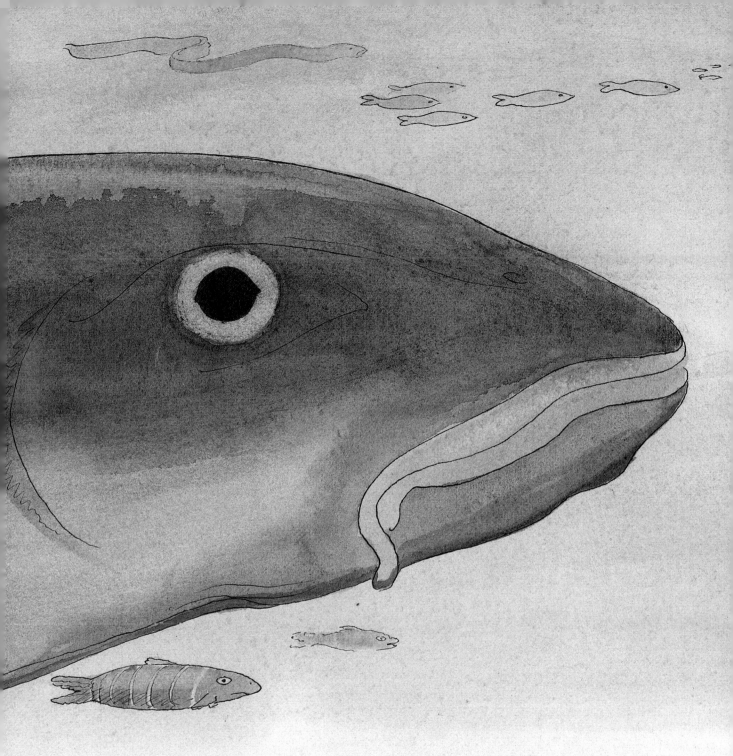

He prayed to the Lord from the great fish's belly, saying, "Lord, help me. You have cast me into the deep. Water stretches for miles around me. Vast waves roll over my head. I am banished from your sight. I will never again disobey your word, if only I can be saved, and from now on I will praise you and give thanks to you."

The Lord heard Jonah and spoke to the great fish. It vomited out Jonah upon the dry land.

Jonah went to Ninevah as the Lord had commanded. And the people of Nineveh gave up their evil ways and believed in the Lord.

THE END